You Can't Eat Your Degree

Combine Your Passions and Philosophies to Create the Story of Your Future

Follow Your Passion!
Tricia Berry

Know Yourself –
Danielle Forget Shield

Tricia Berry & Danielle Forget Shield

You Can't Eat Your Degree

Combine Your Passions and Philosophies
to Create the Story of Your Future

Book artwork by Rick Marron
Editing by Julie Freres Grady

Orders: orders@fidelipublishing.com

Publishers Cataloging-in-Publication Data

Berry, Tricia, Forget Shield, Danielle, 2011-
    You can't eat your degree / Tricia Berry & Danielle Forget Shield -
  1st ed.
    p. cm.
    ISBN: 978-1-60414-452-9 (soft cover)
    ISBN: 978-1-60414-453-6 (ebook)

Printed in the USA

Fideli Publishing, Inc.
119 W. Morgan St.
Martinsville, IN 46151
www.FideliPublishing.com

825 Basics
PO Box 965
Houston, TX 77001
www.825Basics.com

Table of Contents

Acknowledgements

To all the college students we've worked with throughout the past 20 years — you've inspired us, laughed with us and taught us so much about how things continue to change while the basics stay the same.

Thank you to Cecilia Rose, one of Houston's premier executive career coaches, for her suggestions, guidance and inspiration and especially for the clever title of our book. Thank you to Rick Marron, the artist who created our artwork and flip cartoon graphics. And last, but certainly not least, to our editor, Julie Freres Grady whose suggestions greatly improve the delivery of our content.

Before we release our books, we ask a select group of people who are the target audience of the material to review our content. For this book we asked college students and parents of college students for their feedback. Thanks to Mark and Lynn Font, Jordan Keller, Diana Lindsey, Terra, Laura and Jennifer Richardson, Kathryn Sandhop and Linda Tatosian for helping us. We really appreciate your honest and candid feedback.

During our careers we've each had the benefit of an incredible group of BCFs (Best Career Friends). These people have supported us and given us the strength and drive to be better than we ever thought we could on our own. We're grateful for them and hope that you fill your future with people who do the same for you.

Introduction

College is a time for exploration, learning and personal growth. It's also a time to consider your career aspirations and investigate possible career paths. In college you pull from the past and engage in new experiences that help you envision your future. Your vision should include a script of your career story that will help guide your steps along your chosen career path.

Your career story incorporates your strengths, goals, passions and dreams. It is a description of who you are and what you want your future to look like. During college three opportunities you encounter over and over can shape your career story:

1. Ask classmates, professors, managers, alums and others already living it to tell you about their career paths so that you can learn about a wide variety of options. Two people may have the same degree, but very different experiences and career paths throughout college and after graduation.

2. Share information about yourself to give someone else the knowledge and desire to connect you with a potential career, job or other opportunity. You should consider and know how to respond to "Tell me about yourself" to be prepared for opportunities when they arise, such as scholarship applications, job interviews, career fairs and networking events.

3. Determine if you are a good fit for a potential career, graduate school or workplace *and* if it's a good fit for you. Establishing whether a career path would be a good fit is one of the surest ways to achieve both career satisfaction and future success.

Without your story, it's very hard to pinpoint your next step toward your dream job or the perfect path for you. It's also quite difficult for the people who really want to help you find that perfect direction. You need to take charge of your career story — collect your own data, define your own script and communicate it strategically to chart your perfect path.

This book shows you how to use your college experiences as the first steps on your career path. You can't eat your degree. The piece of paper you are handed at graduation won't pay the bills or put food on your table, but how you use your degree to make the life you want can fulfill you in ways you perhaps never considered. Making a difference in our world can provide the sustenance you need.

Describing where you see yourself headed in the future is sometimes challenging. Your future is a story not yet written. As you write your career story, we'd like you to shift perspective — instead of a series of nouns or titles, such as manager or sales associate, think about a collection of adjectives or descriptors, such as creative, detail-oriented, leader or innovator. Think of your career story as having your cake and eating it too. The story includes characters, locations, situations, struggles, successes and so much more.

Throughout *You Can't Eat Your Degree,* we'll challenge you to create a description of what is important to you in your work life, the strengths you want to use, the feelings you want to have, and the impact you need to make as you progress through your college career and along your career path. You'll explore external or outside information and observations from family, friends, acquaintances, coworkers and all others you may interact with. You'll explore the internal or inside, examining characteristics, interests and values that are part of your core and that can signify what is important to you. We'll show you how to start taking note of the career path clues that are outside and inside you.

It may seem like the answer to "What do you want to be when you grow up?" gets harder to answer as you age. Choosing a major in college can seem like a daunting task; and shortly after you pick your major, it's time to think about your career path. Along the way, many people question if they are on the path that best fits their skills and passions. It can feel like an endless cycle of questioning, testing and trying; but it doesn't have to be that way.

This book provides alternatives to the traditional answers for questions like "What do you want to be when you grow up?", "Tell me about yourself." and "What are your five-year goals?" You'll learn how to use the experiences you collect throughout college and the information you already know about yourself to find your dream job and plan and communicate the career path that best fits the real you.

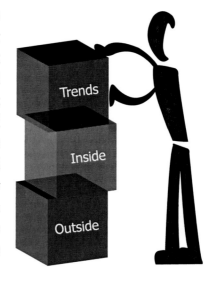

You already have valuable information about yourself, your interests, dislikes and desires. As your education progresses, you will continue to collect information, experiences and understanding. After identifying *outside* and *inside* career path clues, you will begin to spot and compile emerging *trends* among those clues. Once you recognize trends, you can better manage your highs and lows. You can direct yourself to careers and positions that best fit your wants, needs, skills and abilities. You'll discover that next step after graduation and beyond. The descriptions and dialogue you create to script your career story can be used to:

- Identify your dream job and tell a prospective employer exactly why YOU are the perfect candidate

- Demonstrate clear direction and confidence in job interviews and career activities

- Ask the right questions in informational interviews, at career fairs and during job interviews

- Create a compelling essay that tells your future graduate school who you really are.

- Tell your career story using social media where recruiters in your desired field look for candidates.

By the end of the book, perhaps you will be able to eat your degree, as you'll know how to use your degree and experiences to guide your career story to a fulfilling future designed by you especially for you. When you combine your passions and philosophies identified during your college experiences in a coordinated and strategic view, you begin to create the story of your future — one that gives you more than your degree; one that provides the resources to eat!

Our Career Stories

Before we get started, we'd like to introduce ourselves so you know what our stories are and why we wanted you to have the information covered in this book. It is the outside view, inside perspective and career trend information we wish we'd had as we explored our career options in our late high school and college years. Throughout the book, we'll tell you more about our experiences and those of high school and college students we've counseled.

Danielle Forget Shield —

Career and Life Lessons Learned

Danielle didn't know what she wanted to be when she grew up. In high school, she struggled with this quite a bit, but knew she enjoyed and excelled at math and science. One day, when someone asked what she was planning to study in college (for what seemed like the millionth time), she said engineering. Her father is an engineer and it just came out. The reaction was overwhelming — "wow, you must be smart." That's all it took (*outside*). Danielle liked the response she got (*inside*) and just kept saying engineering (*trend*). Danielle was probably more surprised than anyone when she was accepted to some fairly prestigious engineering schools. It all felt like some crazy joke that just wouldn't end. But she didn't have any other direction in mind, so she kept moving forward.

After a couple of years of studying engineering and not doing very well (*trend*), Danielle decided she needed to transfer out of engineering and into something she might be better suited for. She wasn't sure what that would be, but it seemed like her GPA needed resuscitating. Instead, a work-study job manager (*outside*) encouraged her to get a co-op job to see if the practical part of engineering might motivate her to perform better in classes. The co-op job went well and the experience convinced Danielle that she should try a different kind of engineering instead of making a more drastic move (*inside*). That was the first step for Danielle on a long path of self-discovery. Making a slight shift made a tremendous difference — Dean's List different! Danielle was so intrigued by this discovery that she wondered what other small shifts could make big differences (*trend*). She set out on a quest to figure out who she was, what she wanted in a career and how to define it. She sought out and took any opportunity she could to explore her inner self and career story options while she was in college.

Times were tough when Danielle graduated from college. There was a weak economy and high unemployment. Engineering graduates were not getting job offers. In 1994 there weren't internet job postings and recruiting on campus was at a low point. Her career started with effort fueled by an informed career story — 362 mailed resumes that led to 12 interviews and one job offer. Sold! Danielle was excited to have a job, especially one in the specific area she studied, high speed rail. After moving from St. Louis to Houston with great anticipation, Danielle's position lasted about 2 weeks, until the project lost funding (*outside*). Danielle was then transferred to the solid-waste group. That's right, trash. It took about a month and a great manager (*outside*) to turn a really bad attitude into a great career future. Accepting that sometimes things just fall into place for a reason you might not understand was Danielle's next lesson. She realized that her career future was going to be her own responsibility and she dove head-first into learning as much as possible about finding a dream job that could also provide financial freedom. After all, she had about $60,000 in student loans to pay back.

Over the next 15 years, Danielle continued her pursuit of that perfect union between her dream job and financial success. Her path took her through some wonderful jobs and some not-so-great ones. Along the way, she repeated her mantra *Know Yourself*. She continued to read, learn, attend classes, watch others and pay close attention to what motivated her. And the further along her career path that she got, the more she realized that a dream job is a description and not a title. Things will continually change and most of the time you can't control your employer's financial security. You can, however, control your career direction by knowing where you want to go and by communicating your story effectively.

The culmination of this led to Danielle's annual personal trend analysis. She applied engineering principles to career planning: collect your data, analyze your data and use it to choose the next step. That process led her to realize that jumping from a corporate Vice President position into an entrepreneurial role is not that much of a stretch. It's just the next step toward her dream job description; the next chapter in her career story. Danielle gets excited to share the trend analysis process with students because, while you have a world of opportunities ahead of you, that potential can oftentimes seem like a huge weight on your shoulders. Danielle wants to lift that weight using a shortcut she wishes she'd had many years ago — the culmination of 20 years of workshops, books and conferences in one, simple process that will give you the knowledge and confidence to dictate your career story.

Tricia Berry—

What Do You Want to Be When You Grow Up?

Early in her engineering career, Tricia took a course called "Managing Your Career with Power." It was an eye-opening experience that encouraged her to explore her passions, take a look outside and inside herself, examine her trends and define her dream job (*inside*). It was the first time Tricia had taken this overall look at herself and her career trends and really thought about the career story she was crafting. The process in this book has much of its roots in Tricia's resulting journey toward her dream job. It is a process she knows would have been valuable while in college where there are so many more opportunities to explore career options and examine your trends. Had she understood this process or had this book in college, she could have crafted her career story differently in those early years, more closely aligning her passions, interests and strengths with her vision of a dream job.

Looking back now, it's easy to see the trends across Tricia's experiences and to connect them to her passions and dream job. But in college, she was working through her chemical engineering degree, exploring various types of jobs and wondering if she was really in the right major (*inside*). Tricia had chosen engineering because she was good in math and science and her mother had suggested engineering as an option. She'd picked chemical engineering because an advisor at The University of Texas at Austin (UT Austin) had said it was the easiest major to get into as an out-of-state student (*outside*). It wasn't a planned decision and wasn't derived from some deep inner passion for organic chemistry and differential equations.

Tricia ended up liking many of her engineering classes at UT Austin and learned what types of chemical engineering jobs she enjoyed through various co-op positions at The Dow Chemical

Company. Of course, she also learned the classes and types of jobs she really hated and would never want to do for a career. She enjoyed all her extracurricular activities in college, including being a leader in various student organizations for which she organized events and led student teams (*trend*).

Upon graduation, Tricia took a cool job with Dow and immediately got involved in local organizations, community service efforts, school tutoring and more (*trend*). She progressed in her engineering career and took on more and more responsibilities, both at work and in her community engagements. She was recognized for her extracurricular efforts with a number of awards and additional leadership responsibilities. She also heard associates and family comment about the amount of time she invested in *extra stuff* outside her *real* engineering job responsibilities, and had one person say she needed to work on her priorities as it seemed like she always wanted to do the fun stuff first (*outside*).

Today, Tricia has a career that puts all that fun stuff first. After getting an MBA and while working full-time at Dow designing chemical equipment, she began to explore other career options that incorporated more of the fun stuff, such as volunteer interactions, event planning, fundraising, leading teams and educating others (*trend*). With our business, 825 Basics™, she gets to be entrepreneurial, creative and impactful to students and professionals. She gets to apply her engineering problem-solving to career processes and educating others. Concurrently, at UT Austin as the Director of the Women in Engineering Program she gets to be entrepreneurial and creative, and combine that with event planning, fundraising and educating students. She also gets to share her passion for math and science and her love for engineering with others, even though she doesn't actually design chemical equipment anymore.

The trends were there early on. Even in high school Tricia led teams, organized events and loved educating others. She has always enjoyed being creative and her entrepreneurial spirit came through in innovations in her organizations and various jobs. But it wasn't until the "Managing Your Career With Power" class that Tricia put it all together (*inside*). She started crafting her own career story and defining her own career path based on what she knew she enjoyed.

You have the chance to apply this process to your own career path and craft your own career story now. As you read through this book, you'll be able to answer the "Tell me about yourself" question in a way that took Tricia many years to answer. She can now say, "I'm an engineer and educator. I love math and science and I love getting others excited about them too. I am also an entrepreneur and I get to use my creativity and communication skills to help others craft their own career story." By the end of the book, you too will have a better understanding of yourself, a glimpse of your career trends and the beginnings of a script you can use to tell others who you are and where you want to go in your career.

Get Started

You'll probably find that while you are walking across campus, showering after a workout or doodling in class, thoughts and ideas will surface that need to be captured. Make sure you're ready to grab these thoughts. It's these thoughts, experiences and observations that will help you tell your story and design your own career path. In a world of endless options for capturing data, we'll let you determine what works best for you to collect your experiences, understandings and observations. We offer an electronic workbook that can be used with <u>You Can't Eat Your Degree</u> and is downloadable at 825basics.com. Let's get started!

> Download the <u>You Can't Eat Your Degree</u> workbook at 825basics.com to begin collecting your information and creating your career story.

The Authentic, Genuine, Real You

Who are you? You may know who you are, but how do you put it into words? How do you communicate it simply and easily to the thousands of people who will ask "Who are you?" or "What do you do?" When an interviewer says, "Tell me about yourself," can you clearly answer? When you are asked on an application, "What are your strengths?" do you already know what you would want to say? You have to start with the authentic, genuine, real you to answer these questions.

Genuinely understand who you are, what you believe, what you want and know how to communicate it consistently to define you. Do so from an outside and an inside perspective — consider how others perceive you and what you know about yourself. People will see through a façade and it is easier to be true to yourself, genuine, who you truly are, than someone you are not. Combining outside and inside views helps define the real you, crafts your career story and guides your career path.

Look Outside

What do others tell you about yourself? What do you admire in other people? Who challenges you, pushes you to your limits and helps you define what you want to be? This outside image or external view of who you are can provide a new perspective on how to respond to "Tell me about yourself."

This outside perspective includes how others view you and how you view other people. What others have to say about you, your work, or your strengths and weaknesses provides a glimpse of how the real you is perceived. But how you view others — what you respect in them, the characteristics you desire to emulate — partly defines what you value. Feedback people give you, perspectives shared by your mentors and supporters, and what you admire in your role models are outside help in completing the picture of your future, in creating each fulfilling step along your career path.

Pay Attention to Compliments

Consider what others observe about your strengths and skills. What kind of compliments do you consistently receive? Compliments give you a window into other people's positive views of your image or personal brand, the public perception of who you are and what about you is valued.

Pay attention to what people say to you. When someone gives you a compliment, they are affirming a strength they see in you. Compliments come in a variety of forms. You may not recognize compliments until you listen for them. Compliments can be understated and small, such as, "I enjoyed your presentation this morning." And they can be suggestive and large, such as, "You really should run for student body President."

Start noticing when, why and for what others recognize you. Compliments occur frequently, but most of us are too busy to notice. Some people need a reminder to stop and pay attention to the compliments they hear. If this is you, begin to really listen to what others say to you. You will often be surprised at what other people value about you.

Use your workbook to make a list of compliments you have received. Remember to include the small and large ones. What are the compliments that really hit home for you? What compliments make you light up and smile? You'll often seek compliments that are connected to your values or what you view as important in the workplace or in your life. What do your compliments say about your interests or your values?

Examples of Compliments	What They Might Say about You
That was very generous of you.	You are empathetic, think of others, are caring, enjoy giving, feel rewarded best with good feelings or give your time to help
She is the expert in our group.	You work hard, are smart, have a specific skill or understanding of an issue that makes you more valuable than your peers
If anyone ever needs help with that, you are the person to call.	You are open to questions, enjoy sharing your knowledge, value gaining expertise, work hard and well with others, like teaching or are detail-oriented with a flair for explaining things so that anyone can understand
You are a great networker.	You are friendly, outgoing, confident, recognize the need for relationships and recall details about people, are truly interested in hearing their stories or may be genuinely interested in helping others succeed
You are really good at getting things moving in our student organization.	You know where you are headed, have goals, understand how to get started or the details involved, are effective at leading, or enjoy planning, executing or seeing action happen
The <u>You Can't Eat Your Degree Workbook</u> offers more examples.	

The best compliment Danielle gets is when someone says she has done something clever. Clever, to her, is the intersection between creative and intelligent. She goes out of her way to make sure that she does clever things. The flip cartoon motif in this book is used in all of our books and is a result of this. If an accomplishment can be connected to cleverness, Danielle feels really good about it. This was true when she chose engineering as a reaction to someone saying she was smart in high school and carries through in her career story today. She has realized the importance of ensuring that her strengths of cleverness, creativity and intelligence are central to any steps along her career path.

When your compliments and strengths align, you know that you are effectively living your career story and being the best you in the classroom, workplace or other activities. If they do not align, explore ways you can showcase or communicate your strengths and successes to generate compliments, or examine the compliments you receive for strengths you may not have been aware of and strive to demonstrate those more often. We'll discuss exploring your strengths in the section *Looking Inside*.

Listen and pay attention to the compliments you receive and you'll have a very good picture of what strengths those around you see in you and value in you. They will help craft your script for your career path by highlighting those areas you want to note in conversations connected to your career future.

Crafting Gonzalo's Career Story: What could compliments tell Gonzalo about himself – or at least tell him about the image others have of him?

Compliments Gonzalo has received:	Resulting Insight for His Career Story:
• It's great how you can talk to and connect with anyone at any level. • I love your creative and unique solutions. • You are good at generating new ideas and solutions that others don't see. • You have lots of projects going on. It always seems like you are starting something new and innovative.	I value relationships and enjoy exploring new ideas. I'd embrace change and like a dynamic work environment and an organizational culture that appreciates innovation. I am a big-picture person because it's hard to dig into details when you're always thinking about new ideas or starting new projects.

Notate your compliments to unveil insight into your career story using the downloadable workbook. Regularly explore how your compliments can be incorporated in your story.

Consider Comments

Comments are those words that perhaps sting a bit or make you pause to consider how you could have done something differently. What do you hear from those around you? In your past experiences, what areas of improvement have been noted? These types of comments are often made in a light-hearted joking manner, but there is generally some truth in teasing.

There are two sides of comments. While they highlight inherent weaknesses, they also call attention to the things you want to and can improve. Sometimes the comments you hear reflect upon weaknesses in your personality or abilities. No one is perfect. Everyone has areas where they don't excel and will likely never excel. You may also have things you just don't like to do, and so you may have no interest in improving in those areas. If we could all be great at sports, being an Olympian or a super-star athlete wouldn't be that big of a deal. Being aware of your inherent weaker traits and hearing that others agree with your personal perception allows you to identify areas that are not good career paths for you. Danielle is terrible at cooking. She's sure she could work to get better at it, but she doesn't enjoy it. If someone made a comment about her cooking, she'd likely turn it into a joke and let them know how much she dislikes cooking. And she'd remind herself that being a chef is not a career path she should ever consider.

Examples of Comments	What They Might Say about You
With friends like you, who needs enemies?	You are perceived as abrupt, harsh, not concerned about others' input, a gossiper or someone likely to sabotage others
Lighten up, everyone is doing their best.	You have overly high expectations, are impatient, find it hard to share information or responsibilities effectively or are missing the details in the work it takes to make the big picture
Have you thought about taking a class in that area?	You need improvement in a specific area, might not be effectively communicating your knowledge or skills or may need to consider hiring someone else to finish a particular task that is not one of your strengths
Do you need some assistance?	You need help in this area or with this amount of work and are being very expressive with your body language or emotions, or you are appreciated and others want to ease your load
I don't understand what you mean.	Communicating may be a challenge for you or conveying your thoughts effectively to others with a different educational level or expertise
You're not pulling your weight. It would be nice if you'd participate in our project.	You might not care about the outcome but need to contribute to show you are hard working, interested in the success of your group or company and respectful of other people's time and efforts
See the You Can't Eat Your Degree Workbook for additional examples.	

Comments about weaknesses that you can and want to improve are the areas you should explore further in your career. If a comment hurts or makes you feel bad, it may be about an area you value or trait you admire. Comments can give you hints about what you should, or should not, consider as a future career path. You can continue to make improvements, but you can also pursue a different aspect of the same career field that doesn't require the trait as much, or surround yourself with people who compliment your weaknesses.

You may receive some comments that you don't agree with. You don't need to react to every comment you receive, but you should listen to them. Often people might not have all the information they need to make a fair statement. Sometimes perceptions are flawed and serve as an alert that you need to communicate more effectively. There are lots of reasons for comments that you may not perceive as fair, but you should still accept the comments graciously and consider what you could do to change the perception or clear up the situation.

The key in these interactions is your reaction. Once you've received feedback, you must respond positively whether you consider the feedback valuable or think the person is crazy. Remember that the important part of your reaction is understanding what others perceive to be true. If you react harshly or by saying "You're crazy," that person will never give you feedback again. Others will likely hear of your reaction and will reconsider giving you feedback again. Be appreciative, polite and professional — really think about what you have been told.

Some easy ways to respond when you receive feedback are:

- That's a great idea.
- I never thought of that angle.
- I really appreciate your honesty.
- I appreciate your expertise in this area.
- I always learn something from talking with you.

Even if you don't agree with the feedback, acknowledge it and thank the person for sharing with you. The perspective you can gain from listening to the comments people make adds to the story you are creating of your future. Remember to pay attention to the way you react. Your reactions can tell you how much you care about an issue. Use this to help determine aspects you may want to incorporate in your career story.

Crafting Lola's Career Story: What could comments tell Lola about herself or the image others have of her?

Comments Lola has received:	Resulting Insight for Her Career Story:
• Can't stand those meetings, can you? • You should participate more in the team discussions. • Writing isn't your thing, is it? • Do you need help with our homework?	I'm really not very good at hiding my feelings if they are so obvious to others, but being genuine is important to me. I'm just not as comfortable in large group settings. Communicating is a challenge if it must be in writing. I prefer to work alone and do not want to participate in meetings, teams or even seek help for homework.

Detail your comments feedback to discover more about yourself for your career story using the downloadable workbook. Regularly explore how comments can enhance your story.

Know Your Career Image

Your career image is the view others have of you and how they perceive your work. In college, this career or professional image may have a classroom or student organization setting. It's the view your professors, advisors and classmates have of your college work, such as your homework, projects and student organization activities.

Your career image is something you begin to influence in college. You can choose what you want your image to be and take steps to make it become a reality. College is the perfect time to decide how you want to be perceived. The high school image of you is gone and the college and career image of you is ready to be defined. You establish a reputation with your professors, the administrators, recruiters and all of your fellow students. And this image you choose to display can tell you a lot about yourself and what you value.

Like most college students, Danielle was required to participate in several faculty assigned class team projects. A member of one of these teams did not participate at all. He knew that the rest of the group wanted to maintain their GPAs and were committed to an A-level project, so, he gambled on the fact that the rest of the team would pick up his slack to ensure a high grade. The reputation he developed with the rest of his teammates was that he was self-centered and lazy. Almost 20 years later, Danielle doesn't recall the names of the other high-performers on that team. But she does recall the slacker. If his resume ever came across her desk or if she was asked if she knew him, she'd certainly have something to share.

What is your career image? How do others perceive you and your work? Does your image match the one you desire? Consider the following questions to understand and define your image:

- When people meet you, what is their first impression?

- When people work with you on a project, how do they describe you to others?

- What is it you want people to say about you?

- How can you convey your career image through your appearance and interactions?

Use your workbook or other means to capture both the image you want others to have of you and the answers to these questions.

Crafting Randy's Career Story: What could career image descriptors tell Randy about himself, or about the image others have of him?

How people describe Randy's career image:	Resulting Insight for His Career Story:
- Successful, driven and headed toward success at any cost - Focused on the prize – a BIG salary with bonus' and lots of benefits - The life of the party after hours, but a very different person in class - Sucks up to the professors and staff to make sure he gets what he wants - Knows where to get the answers - Pulled together – always looks like he could walk into an interview, even when playing sports	I value success and hard work, and I want results. Salary and status are tied to success for me. I am confident and not afraid to seek out what I need or desire, as is evident in my interactions with professors and others' observations about my being focused and driven. I desire control and being at the center of the attention in class or work and in play.

List your career image descriptors to identify your image or brand for your career story using the downloadable workbook. Regularly explore how your career image impacts your story.

Just remember that everything you do creates an image for the outside world. You might not be very concerned with this concept now, but it could greatly impact your future. What you do in class, how you interact in student organizations and how you portray yourself online can all have an effect on the career or professional image others have of you. You want that image to align with your future career path rather than create stumbling blocks or career limiting information. Your career image is your personal brand, yours to define. Don't just let it happen; make it happen.

Understand Role Models

Compliments, comments and descriptions of your career image may be taken more seriously if you hear them from someone you admire, look up to or respect. Role models are those people you look to as a positive example. They have a career image you desire and want to emulate.

Understanding who your role models are and why you consider them to be role models can provide you with insights into your own values and interests. Any job you seek or experience you collect should align with these values and interests. They should be considered when charting your career path and telling your career story.

One of Danielle's role models is a former colleague whose positive attitude about everyone and everything made him a pleasure to work with. When a situation erupted and most coworkers turned to a blame-and-complain mode, he jumped into problem-solving. If someone said "Bob doesn't know what he's doing. He really messed that up." This person would say "Maybe Bob has some family issues we don't know about, so let's assume he's just having a bad day and help him fix it." Danielle was continually struck by this person's positive attitude and she continues to strive to emulate him. She values his ability to stay positive and to look at all sides of an issue, and hopes that she displays the same quality throughout her career.

Identify the people you admire and consider as role models. Some of the people on your list will be a part of your college life, some may be a part of your past and others might be people you just know in passing. You may include family members, friends, managers, coaches, professors or advisors as role models. The important part is to clearly identify what it is you admire about them. What characteristics do these people have that make them role models? Is it their job, their lifestyle, the impact they've had on a specific issue or group of people? Is it the way they act or treat others? Is it a skill they have or a way they go about their interactions, relationships, work or play?

Once you've identified what you admire about each person, ask yourself why you admire that trait. Continue to ask yourself why until you clearly define what it is about that person that appeals to you. What about that person do you want to be a part of your story? Understanding your role models and how their characteristics tie to your values and interests gives you a better understanding of yourself. Capture your role models and which traits you want to emulate in your workbook.

Crafting Estela's Career Story: What could these role model characteristics tell Estela about what she wants to emulate?

What Estela admires about her role models:	Resulting Insight for Her Career Story:
• Janet is able to lead without being loud or obnoxious or making anyone feel bad. • People really seem to like being around Brian because he is so genuine and giving of his time and knowledge. • Professor Perkins makes class fun and explains complicated material in simple terms. He seems to really care that every person in the class has learned something. • Mrs. Finkelstein has a family and a successful career and seems to have it all figured out. • Sarah Jessica Parker — talk about staying power! She takes breaks between celebrity events and work to be a real person and enjoy time with her family.	I believe people's feelings are important and that it is important to consider your impact on others through your words and actions. I value helping others and balancing work and family. I want to be around people who are genuine and compassionate. I could be happiest by seeking a career setting where helping people or inspiring others is a central function.

Identify your role models and what you admire about them to know which characteristics you should include in your career story using the downloadable workbook. Regularly explore how your role models impact your story.

Identify Mentors and BCFs

Your mentors are those go-to people who can offer advice about your coursework, activities and future. They may be professors, advisors, managers, relatives or classmates. They can serve as advocates for you and can provide feedback about your work, your image or career path. Your mentors can help you stay aware of opportunities to demonstrate strengths or find that perfect job. They provide direct feedback and guidance and can hold you accountable to your goals. Should your activities or direction drift from your path, your mentors can call you on it and help you correct your perceptions or course of action. They are able to help tell your career story and share your accomplishments with others to create new opportunities or career paths for you.

One of the mentors Tricia had in college was the advisor for one of her student organizations. He was a respected faculty member, enthusiastic educator and fabulous communicator — all characteristics Tricia admired. Tricia was an officer in the organization and interacted with the advisor on a regular basis. He was able to observe Tricia's leadership, communication and organizational skills. He noticed Tricia's event planning and collaboration strengths and provided compliments and other feedback during their interactions. The advisor encouraged Tricia to continue honing these skills and recommended her to lead a regional conference for the organization. He helped Tricia craft her career story to include organizational skills, something she may not have considered without the advisor's guidance.

Danielle became very involved with the Society of Women Engineers (SWE) when she was in college. She took full advantage of building relationships whenever possible with the professional members in the St. Louis area where she attended college. While Danielle was in college, the national SWE President happened to be from St. Louis and was someone she had developed a relationship with during these professional association interactions. Developing a mentoring relationship with someone in a successful career was not only personally rewarding, but led to interviews with the mentor's company that otherwise would not have been possible.

Mentors are great and absolutely necessary for your future success. But the other group of advocates and reality-checkers you should begin developing while in college, Best Career Friends (BCFs), will challenge you, support you, struggle with you and push you farther than you would have gone on your own. They often know your history and personal situation and can provide a perspective that a mentor might not have. They may be friends you have through your student organizations, past bosses with whom you have a good working relationship or even high school friends. They have enough distance from you to have some outsider perspective, but are close enough to you to more earnestly understand who you are and what you are about.

As you progress through college and your career, you will hopefully find both mentors and BCFs to help you craft your career story. Seek them to provide some observations you may not have recognized yourself. Danielle values the guidance, support and opinions of both her mentors and BCFs as she moves along her career path. She has frequently struggled with choosing the corporate or entrepreneurial path, and sometimes felt the corporate opportunities were too good to pass up. While she has consulted her mentors about the opportunities along her corporate path, Danielle does not necessarily introduce her entrepreneurial goals into the discussions.

With her mentors, she focuses on the opportunity at hand and whether it is a good career fit. When she talks with her BCFs, they often ask very different questions about career choices. They want to know how this corporate position will prepare Danielle for her ultimate entrepreneurial endeavor. And once she's accomplished a personal goal, her BCFs are pushing her to the next one. These honest reminders have greatly enhanced Danielle's career and have helped her stay on track to accomplish her ideal career path. They've challenged her to create bigger and better goals and accomplish more. The company Tricia and Danielle co-founded, 825 Basics, would not exist if these BCFs hadn't been there to encourage its formation. When she considers or begins a new adventure in her career story, Danielle goes to her mentors first to seek guidance. Then, her BCFs keep her on track with her new role and objectives and remind her of her goals when she loses sight of her path.

Take a few minutes to identify your mentors and BCFs. Consider who helps you now and who provides feedback or career suggestions. Think of who knows the real you and understands your goals and career story. Decide if there are others within your networks with whom you would like to develop a deeper relationship. Consider seeking out and adding new mentors who may be able to fill in the gaps and provide you with feedback on other areas of your future. Use your workbook to capture this information.

Crafting Ralph's Career Story: What could this advice from mentors and BCFs tell Ralph about his career path?

Advice from Ralph's mentors and BCFs regarding his experiences and career path:	Resulting Insight for His Career Story:
<ul><li>You've got to find something that really lets you explore.</li><li>It seems like money isn't a motivator for you.</li><li>I really notice how much you enjoy your summers off for self-exploration.</li><li>Backpacking through South America on your own was quite brave.</li><li>You seem to really enjoy your classes and spending time on research.</li></ul>	I might consider exploring a career that allows for flexible work time or sabbaticals. I may work best in an organization that values continued learning and research. The journey (self-exploration, South America, research) is more important than the end result (money, working through summers). An organization and people who value the journey may be a great fit for me on my career path.

Seek input from mentors and BCFs to inform your career story and record that input using the downloadable workbook. Regularly explore what your mentors and BCFs see in you and your possibilities for furthering your career story.

Your mentors and BCFs know the authentic, genuine, real you and can provide the external perspective you may need to stay true to your career story. They can help you craft your script, define next steps on your career pathway and promote your career story to others.

Developing Mentor and BCF Relationships

Identifying mentors and best career friends (BCFs) during college and early in your career can be difficult, but is extremely rewarding. Try these tips to develop such relationships as early as possible:

- Join professional organizations that align with your major and participate in activities to meet members already working in your chosen industry. Take advantage of activities to gain BCFs among other student members, as well as mentors in established, professional members.

- Engage professors, coaches and university staff. Visit during office hours to ask questions about their career choices and those of students they have mentored. This is a great way to develop mentor relationships..

- Use alumni directories to find mentor and BCF advocates. You may be astonished to learn how many alumni are willing to help you in any way they can, but calling to ask for a job upon graduation is not the way to use this resource. Develop relationships with alumni who work in your field of study early in your college years to have established mentors in place long before graduation arrives and at key milestones on your career path.

- Participate in volunteer activities that allow you to meet a wide variety of people. Your BCFs do not need to be in your field of study. In fact, finding supporters with other perspectives can be incredibly beneficial in your future. Every industry relies on expanded sets of skills...engineers must be able to write reports and writers need to be able to calculate return on investment.

Generate Outside Input

Looking outside provides a magnifying glass to see things you may have never noticed before. Tricia received a comment from someone she considered a mentor and role model. He had noticed that she liked to do the *fun stuff* first. That simple comment gave Tricia a new perspective causing her to really evaluate what the *fun stuff* was, why she did it first and how others perceived her priorities. This eventually led to Tricia shifting her career path to more closely align with what she was most skilled at and enjoyed. The view from the outside gave Tricia the perspective she needed to make the transition and, ultimately, align her career story more closely with her values, passions and strengths.

If you don't feel like you receive compliments or other feedback, you need to find a way to generate some. Having an outside view is important and sometimes you need to take the initiative to generate such data. This can take time and can require a shift in your surroundings. Some environments just don't seem to foster feedback, but you can change that by trying these techniques:

- Give compliments to others

- Solicit feedback when an event occurs
- Use online survey tools to allow for soliciting anonymous feedback to make people feel more comfortable
- Ask specific, but open-ended questions for full answers instead of yes/no responses
- Recognize that most people are not comfortable giving feedback, let alone directly, and that doesn't necessarily say something about you
- Accept feedback, whether positive or negative, with appreciation and a positive response to let people know you really want feedback and plan to use it.

Many people are uncomfortable asking for feedback. Here are some simple ways to ask for feedback in a variety of situations:

Situation	Sample Question
Presentation	I felt like people struggled with the information in my presentation today. What could I have done to make the information easier to understand?
Meeting	I wasn't getting much feedback in our officer meeting today. Were the ideas I presented clear? What could I do to improve the meetings?
Document Review	I presented the information in a new format to make the numbers clearer. Did that help make our proposal easier to understand? I really want our advisor to approve this project.
Casual Fridays	I'm struggling with business casual. You always look very professional. Do you have any tips on how to enhance my wardrobe to appear more professional?
Classroom	Professor Watkins doesn't seem to value the ideas I share in class. Do you have any thoughts on how I can communicate my ideas more effectively?
Networking Event	You seem to know many people in our department. Do you have tips on how I can start building my own network of mentors?

These examples provide you with a framework that can be applied to many situations. Some subjects are much more difficult to approach. Just practice saying it with a friend, advisor or coworker before you use it. Practice in front of the mirror, on your walk, ride or drive to school or work. The more you say something out loud, the more comfortable and apt you'll be using it when needed. It's important to ask for feedback at work, school and extracurricular activities. You need that outside view to help define your career story and if you don't ask for feedback, you may never get it!

Considering the compliments you receive, the comments you hear and the characteristics you admire in your role models, and learning through mentors and BCFs helps to craft the picture of the genuine you. Paying attention to the information you hear from those around you adds even more value and introduces descriptors you might not have considered for your career story.

Look Inside

The outside view gives one perspective about your image and the authentic, genuine, real you. But before you can tell someone who you are or what you want to do with your future, career and life, you must also look inside yourself, exploring characteristics, mindsets, dreams and more. By provoking new career thoughts, looking at yourself in a different way, and considering the inside view in addition to outside perspectives, you will begin to take charge of and clarify a definition of the genuine you.

The pictures you like or share of yourself generally capture more than your physical image. They capture your personality, what makes you smile, what you enjoy, your aspirations, your friends, your feelings and, likely, your future. It's the real you that shines through in pictures. And it's this real you that can be used to help define and refine where you are headed. Your career story incorporates what you tell people about yourself, what you believe about yourself, the activities you like or dislike, and your strengths and weaknesses. It's this real you and the career story you are scripting that combine with your degree to set you on your best, fulfilling career path.

Introduce Yourself

When you meet someone for the first time, how do you introduce yourself? Do you introduce yourself differently in class, in an interview, at a club meeting or at a party? It may vary based on the situation, but your introduction defines you. It represents who you are and how you see yourself. Your introduction tells people what you *want* them to know about you at that given time and place. It provides a framework for a first impression and sets the stage for the conversation to follow. Pay attention to how you introduce yourself to your friends, your professors, potential employers, professionals you network with, your friends' families and anyone else you encounter.

- What do you include in your introduction?
- How do you portray yourself to others?
- What does your introduction say about who you are?
- What does your introduction say about what is important to you?

You'll often find that consistent trends appear in how you introduce yourself, regardless of the situation or people involved. Danielle found that as a college student, she was compelled to work into the conversation that she was an engineering student. Even when she continued her education by pursuing a Master of Business Administration (MBA), she continued to include engineer as part of her introduction. Her appearance and attitude were not what you would have initially suspected from an engineering student, but she still wanted people to know that she was smart. So, subconsciously she made sure to tell people what she wanted them to know, what she valued about herself and wanted others to see. This also demonstrates a trend that we've identified for Danielle — she consistently values smart as a core component of her sense of self and her career story.

4 Key Components of an Introduction

⊙ First Name

⊙ Last Name

⊙ Affiliation (e.g., Organization, University, Department, Major, Residence Hall)

⊙ Position (e.g., President, Senior, Graduate Assistant, Residence Hall Floor)

Begin to pay attention to what you say to others in your introduction. What are you compelled to share with others when you first meet them? What you say about yourself in an introduction or in those "Tell me about yourself" moments tells people what you value about yourself and, perhaps, what you value in others. Use your workbook to take the time to prepare and record your introduction. Recording your introduction gives you the opportunity to evaluate what you are saying about yourself, break it down, and identify what you value through the words you use and the information you include. Exploring what you share will give you insights that will prove useful as you narrow your career path.

Crafting Joe's Career Story: What might his introduction characteristics say about himself?

What Joe shares when introducing himself:	Resulting Insight for His Career Story:
• Is a Junior majoring in journalism at ABC University • Enjoys cycling and running • Involved in drawing and writing for the school newspaper • Loves comic books • Volunteers for Habitat for Humanity	I may be interested in a company that creates and invokes the same sense of pride I have experienced in my school. I like seeing immediate results of work – cycling and running give immediate accomplishments, a newspaper offers a quick turnaround on my writing, and volunteering with Habitat for Humanity allows me to see the house construction happening. I am creative, artistic, imaginative and visual. I may work well in a role where I can contribute creatively as an individual. I need an organization that values loyalty and recognizes immediate results.

Consider how you want to introduce yourself in a variety of situations. Write it down or record it in the downloadable workbook to regularly ensure that what you present to others matches your career story. Identify what you consistently tell others about yourself.

Recognize Your Mindsets

A mindset is your guiding attitude, that belief that gives you an instinctual response in any given situation. What mindsets do you have from experiences in school, at home or in life that are guiding you in college and toward a career path?

Tricia had a mindset in college that she had to graduate from the chemical engineering program she chose in her freshman year. She had a finish-what-you-start and persist-until-the-end mindset. During her first couple of years in college, she wasn't thrilled with her classes and her first co-op job in chemical engineering was not exciting. Still, she was doing well in school and did well in her first engineering job, but she just couldn't envision a life as a chemical engineer down the road. Her mindset, however, drove her to graduate with a chemical engineering degree. She never considered changing her major and was fortunate to end up enjoying later engineering classes and jobs, and having a successful career as a chemical engineer. Her mindset had driven her toward graduation and success, and continues to lead her in many of her efforts today. They are part of her career story and continue to help define her career path.

Examples of Mindsets	What They Might Say about You
Education is power	• You are intelligent and value others who are intelligent. • You have a sense of social standing or worth that comes with hierarchy. • You feel compelled to have an education before success can follow.
Work is a means to an end	• You value free time, resting your mind or body and other activities outside of work. • Your dream job may not afford your dream lifestyle.
I can do anything I set my mind to	• You are focused, driven and compelled to prove you can do what is set before you. • You may miss the joy in situations because you are so focused on the end result.
Elders are always right	• You are loyal to hierarchy and systems. • You value experience more than learned knowledge. • You feel a sense of fate or a higher power driving goals rather than personal persistence.
There is no room for second best	• For you, personal excellence is most important. • You are likely to be focused, driven, but may not enjoy many activities because you are afraid to fail.
Finish what you started	• You may not be able to accept change very easily. • You feel challenged with long-term activities because the end is not immediately in sight.
See the <u>You Can't Eat Your Degree Workbook</u> for additional examples.	

What are your mindsets? Think about the beliefs you have about your future. Listen for any absolutes you state when talking with your friends or arguing points in class. We all come from very different family, education, career, world and life mindsets. How are your mindsets shaping your definition of success and your perception of a future career path? Understanding your mindsets enables you to incorporate them into your career story.

Crafting Rebecca's Career Story: What could her mindsets tell Rebecca about herself?

Rebecca has multiple mindsets:	Resulting Insight for Her Career Story:
• Success is an A in every class. • A few close friends are essential. • Fun is something I'll have when I graduate. I'll have plenty of time to relax then. • I can have it all - this is the 21st century!	I am very driven and will work hard to reach my definition of success. I push myself and don't seem to value taking breaks or slowing down. I may have lots of friends and people I associate with in class or student organizations, but I value close relationships with a narrow group of people. I work best in a large organization where I can interact with many and develop deeper relationships with a few. I would also fit well in a goal-driven organization that values or recognizes people who work hard and push themselves.

Examine your mindsets by recording them in the downloadable workbook. Periodically consider what your mindsets tell you about yourself and your career story.

Envision Your Dream Job

One fun and insightful technique for framing your future is to think about your dream job — that job you envision as ideal, perfect and fulfilling. What does your dream job look like? Current life influences may impact what it looks like today, but your dream job will probably change over time. Still, defining what your dream job looks like now can lead to more strategic conversations about your career path with career counselors or in interviews. Knowing your dream job helps you craft your career story and sheds light on the skills you need to hone or develop, and the steps you may need to take you there.

Take some time to think about your ideal situation and dream job. Create a drawing of it, make notes about the aspects of it or use the exercise provided in the workbook to help you consider its characteristics. Whichever method you use, capture the first things that come to mind rather than overanalyzing what you think you should write down. Think about dream job traits such as:

- Job Title
- Location
- Commute
- Work Hours
- Office Space
- Compensation
- Amenities
- Coworkers
- Culture
- Attire
- Management
- Type of Business

- Type of Job
- Learning Opportunities
- Responsibilities
- Travel
- Growth Opportunities
- Social Environment

Detailing your vision of your dream job will help you ask the right questions as you explore career options. For example, in an informational interview where you are learning about a company or a type of job, you might say: "I really enjoy working outside. Are there aspects of your career that allow you to work outside?" You can begin to learn how available jobs and job skills align with the dream job you desire. You can set your sights on a path toward your dream job and understand the language you need to use to share it with others so they can also see your vision.

Tricia had an early career opportunity to take a class called, "Managing Your Career with Power." The most powerful session of the class for her was the dream job and dream lifestyle exercise where she drew out her vision of the future — her house, her community, her workplace, her job. She was told to just clear her mind, then draw and write to see what flowed out of her. What Tricia drew looked nothing like what she was doing and she was shocked.

She was in an engineering job doing engineering projects. She was married and owned her own home in a nice family community. But that wasn't what she drew! She did draw a picture of a house with a family, a couple of kids added in with her husband. But she also drew a picture of herself in front of an easel with people sitting around it like she was teaching them. Her aha moment wasn't the family picture, but the shocking educational aspect of the job she drew. She realized that the extracurricular things she enjoyed doing focused on education. Education was core to her interests, excited her and drove her forward.

Tricia began to envision a future job where education could be central to her responsibilities. She set herself on a path toward that vision, developing the skills and networks needed to move her closer to her dream job. She also began to shift her career story around education, her skills and experiences in this area, her passion for it, and her desired future within the field. Now she is a successful entrepreneur in education as well as a university educator and trainer, educating every day. She may yet have another dream job after this one, but developing that first picture of a perfect career has continued to guide her skills development, communications, decisions and career story.

Keep in mind that like your hopes and desires, your dream job can change over time. Situations change and priorities change, and that's okay. It's important to recognize those consistent traits of your dream jobs over time, and to recognize when your ideal has shifted so that you can shift your career story and path with it.

When she graduated from college, Danielle's dream job was wearing a suit to work in her fancy corporate office and eventually running the company as CEO. She set herself on the path to this ideal and incorporated the vision into her career story. Danielle continually took higher level positions, following her chosen career path. She rounded out her skills set to ensure that she was corporate executive office caliber by gathering experiences in all areas of her industry, obtaining an MBA, and continually working on managerial and soft skills. However, the closer her dream job came to reality, the more she realized she would have to balance the requirements of a corporate position with her current lifestyle, which included family and personal goals.

Danielle realized that the tangible characteristics she associated with career success as a college student and young professional were not what made her happy as a seasoned professional and conflicted with blossoming family priorities. So her dream job title changed, but her career story stayed the same. For now, Danielle's dream job description is to be a successful entrepreneur, another kind of chief, and she continues to redefine her definition of success to fit what works well within her current life situation.

Crafting Sooni's Career Story: What could her dream job characteristics tell Sooni about herself?

Sooni's dream job incorporates many characteristics:	Resulting Insight for Her Career Story:
<ul><li>Job Title - Creative Consultant</li><li>Location - near a beach, preferably in Australia</li><li>Commute - not farther than I can walk or ride my bike</li><li>Work Hours - flexible; I need to be able to catch the waves when they come in</li><li>Office Space - home or a coffee shop; I'm jealous of all the people working at Starbucks</li><li>Compensation - needs to be six figures or I can't afford my lifestyle</li><li>Amenities - sabbaticals, comfy furniture, good coffee</li><li>Coworkers - easy to work with, fun, accepting</li><li>Culture - open and honest</li><li>Attire - surf wear, or close to it</li><li>Management - understanding, recognizes the value of my creativity, flexible</li><li>Type of Business - graphic design</li><li>Type of Job - full-time, but on my terms</li><li>Learning Opportunities - conferences, classes, online courses and webinars</li><li>Responsibilities - lots, I'll run the place in five or six years</li><li>Travel - 50% or more, but only to cool places</li><li>Growth Opportunities - learning, challenges, I'm definitely moving up the ladder</li><li>Social Issues - need to accept me for me</li></ul>	I value freedom and flexibility in my work environment as described in my dream job's hours and management characteristics. The option of telecommuting at least part-time would be ideal for me. I am creative, very competent and leadership-worthy given my dream job title and responsibilities. I work best in a comfortable and casual environment where others are nonjudgmental and perhaps also creative. I want to be encouraged to advance my knowledge in my field, including having the support of senior leadership to attend and present at conferences or through eLearning. I may thrive as an entrepreneur or in an organization that has an entrepreneurial spirit.

Explore the characteristics of your dream job often. Note changes that occur as time passes and life priorities change, continuously updating what your dream job sounds like in the downloadable workbook to ensure your career story keeps track with you.

Understanding your dream job characteristics can help you better understand the best career path for you. It will help you uncover what you are looking for in an organization or job, and can help you craft the questions you ask for feedback as you consider steps, jobs and organizations along your career path. Your dream job vision can provide clues to what you like or dislike and can help provide direction or motivation for your career story.

Identify Likes and Dislikes

The things you do, the jobs and tasks that attract and excite you, and the activities you gravitate toward likely have some things in common that typically extend across projects, volunteer roles and extracurricular activities. Exploring your likes and dislikes helps provide a framework for better understanding yourself and the environment in which you thrive.

Danielle has what most people would consider an odd like. She's noticed that all the jobs she has enjoyed throughout college and her professional career have bottled water cooler dispensers available for employees. The jobs she hasn't liked have not. It may just be a coincidence, but bottled water is something she looks for in a workplace now. If an organization does not have a dispenser, Danielle may still take the job if it's a good one and the right fit, but it signifies that her prospective employer has taken a small step to make things more convenient and to better the environment by taking steps to lessen use of individual water bottles.

She knows that thus far, the jobs she has enjoyed have had this commonality and she pays attention to it as she considers other positions. She has also spoken with other people who have similar likes but other specifics, such as real glassware and a dishwasher to avoid throwing away paper cups. We all have our unique likes and dislikes, and finding a workplace that respects those perspectives is a part of identifying your career path.

Investigating your likes and dislikes in volunteer or extracurricular settings is equally insightful for your ideal workplace. The insight provided can help you identify environments that will allow you to succeed. You are drawn to those situations, tasks, environments and people you expressly like within volunteer or extracurricular settings. If you didn't like the task, you would not be volunteering. You need a variety of outlets to hone your skills, grow your networks and meet your personal needs. Which volunteer activities do you choose to participate in on or off campus? Do they involve athletics or religion? What do these interests define about you?

Many years ago, Tricia participated in an exercise where she mapped her likes and dislikes across various segments of her life, including work, family, volunteer, health and school. The instructor had the class make a list of their extracurricular activities. Tricia was amazed at the length of her list — local grade-school tutor, community service coordinator, event coordinator, recruiter, sports club participant, graduate student, national conference committee chair, local math competition chair, and on and on. Next the instructor shared a bit of information Tricia will never forget, "If you are not getting what you need at work, you will seek it elsewhere." She was seeking everything elsewhere. Her likes were all outside of her job. It was eye opening! From that point forward, Tricia refocused her career path toward her likes and transitioned to a new career that feels like an extracurricular activity every day. Recognizing what you seek outside of the classroom can tell you a lot about your future. Tricia has shared this advice with many people who are in similar situations.

Keep in mind that likes and dislikes are not the same as strengths and weaknesses. You can be great at a task, but hate it. You can love a task, but be awful at it. Be open about what you like and dislike as you investigate a current job, previous jobs, and volunteer or extracurricular activities.

Danielle was a roller-skating carhop at Sonic® when she was in high school. She loved interacting with the customers. Today one of her favorite vacations each year is visiting a friend who owns an ice cream store. She loves working at the ice cream store and talking with all the customers. She has a desire to interact with a variety of people every day. It was apparent when she was 16 years old and continues to be apparent today. People interaction is a central aspect of Danielle's career story.

As you move through your days, use your workbook to note the things you like and dislike about your classes, activities and current or former part-time, summer or co-op jobs. Be open to what you find out — no issue is too small or too large when examining your career motivations.

Examples of Likes and Dislikes	What These Might Say about You
Likes small settings or Dislikes working in large teams	You don't want to be around a lot of people, find comfort in quiet reflection, work best by yourself or prefer focused introspective work
Likes autonomy or Dislikes micromanagement	You are independent, confident, understand the details, may thrive in an entrepreneurial setting or feel insulted when not valued for creativity or innovation
Likes social activities or Dislikes working independently for long periods of time	You are a sociable person who enjoys large groups and may be great at sales or communications, may thrive in a fast paced, changing and exciting environment, likes things to move quickly or prefers short-term activities
Likes frequent interaction with manager/professor or Dislikes not feeling supported	You crave feedback, need clear direction, like recognition and lack confidence in specific areas
See the <u>You Can't Eat Your Degree Workbook</u> for additional examples.	

Tricia's first job was at a Putt-Putt™ golf course where she worked the front counter and snack shop. She was also the birthday party captain for which she scheduled, organized and managed all the birthday parties. Tricia loved organizing and running the parties. She enjoyed all the logistics of setting up the parties and providing a fantastic birthday experience for the kids and families. What she disliked was closing out the cash register at the end of her shift. When Tricia looks back on that first job and characteristics of other volunteer and paid experiences she has enjoyed in her career, she sees the common thread of organization, logistics and creating positive experiences for others. The likes from Tricia's first job are still true to her likes today and she still dislikes the accounting end of things.

Crafting Jackson's Career Story: What could his likes and dislikes tell Jackson about himself?

Jackson's likes include:	Resulting Insight for His Career Story:
• Short commute • Friendly co-workers • Challenging work • Feeling like I make a difference • Computer modeling • Manager in another city • Small office **Jackson's dislikes include:** • Having to spend weekends with my co-workers' families • Limited vacation • Feeling under-paid • An overbearing manager • Being reprimanded for personal use of computer while at work • Repetitive work	I want to work with people who respect and challenge me. I have little patience for situations I can't control, such as traffic and large-office settings. I value freedom and personal time, and would thrive in an environment where work hours are more regular or confined to a typical 40-hour work week. I enjoy more creative, varied and innovative work. I also enjoy being trusted to get my work done and not being micromanaged for how my time is spent if that is happening. Trust my abilities and trust me to do the job right.

List your likes and dislikes in the downloadable workbook, ensuring that you cover work or task related details, but allowing for other, potentially distant life likes and dislikes to soundly inform your career story. Remember to revisit these. The likes and dislikes of your career story may originate from your very first job and volunteer experiences like they did for both of us, but they may morph and expand, twisting and turning as you progress through your college and career experiences. Understanding them and incorporating them into your script can ensure your career path is more fulfilling with fewer dislikes and more enjoyment.

Acknowledge Strengths and Weaknesses

One of the most dreaded and common interview questions is "What are your strengths and weaknesses?" If you have been through an interviewing workshop, you likely learned how to spin your weaknesses into strengths. We want you to explore what you are good at — consider a true strength, not what you spin from a weakness in an interview, but what you really do well. Incorporating the strengths you enjoy into your career story ensures your career path is in alignment with who you are. Just as with your likes, the more of your strengths that can be incorporated into your future career, the more fulfilling you'll find it to be.

You may have physical, mental, analytical reasoning or communication strengths, or strengths in other areas. Consider your personality strengths, your knowledge base or your area of expertise. What do you bring to your teams, school projects or volunteer organizations? Be open about your strengths. No strength is too small or too large when examining your career motivations. Remember that strengths don't have to be something you enjoy; they're simply what you do repeatedly well.

An easy way to determine what strengths others see in you is to look at what tasks you are assigned or asked to perform. Start paying attention to the functions other people ask you to do. You are generally asked to repeat things that others perceive you do well.

Examples of Strengths	What These Say about You
Loyal to organization	You have pride for the products or reputation of your organization, enjoy a sense of community and belonging and need a workplace with ethical, upstanding practices that make you proud
Organized	You thrive in an environment where neatness and order are valued because you are methodical and like when there is a process to follow
Generating enthusiasm	You are inspired within an environment that allows people's passions to shine through and may prefer a workplace that allows for more social interaction
Collaboration	You work best in a less hierarchical organization with lots of interaction across departments because you value teamwork and enjoy working together toward a common goal
Managing people	You are great at delegation, are able to see the details in a project that can be shared responsibilities and are effective at getting things done
See the <u>You Can't Eat Your Degree Workbook</u> for additional examples.	

Working within your strengths typically energizes you and creates a more fulfilling experience. By investigating your strengths and how they connect to your dream job and desired career path, you can begin to craft the career story and the right response to "What are your strengths?"

Crafting Clara's Career Story: What could her strengths tell Clara about herself?

Clara's strengths include:	Resulting Insight for Her Career Story:
• Public speaking • Professional appearance and presence • Ability to make the most technical topic something everyone can understand • Quickly becoming an expert in environmental water quality issues • Really fast at typing • Tech-savvy and finds new devices as easy to use • Great sister, supportive friend, trusted co-worker	My strengths may indicate that I like to be in the spotlight and would thrive in roles where I get to be the face of the organization. I may enjoy being the person people go to for help or advice given my technical expertise and relationships with others. This may also indicate that I have a genuine interest in relationship-building and would work well in a setting where I get to educate others. I may also prefer a professional setting where appearances matter and a commanding public presence and knowledge base are valued.

Craft your career story incorporating your strengths. Regularly update and record them in your downloadable workbook. Periodically self-reflect on these strengths to help ensure you live up to your potential.

You'll need to do the same for your weaknesses. Considering your weaknesses as part of your career story ensures your career path is aligned with who you are. Just as with your dislikes, the fewer of your weaknesses that are incorporated into your future career, the more fulfilling it will be.

Again, a dreaded and common interview question is, "What are your weaknesses?" What do you struggle with? What is an area you feel needs improvement? Just like with strengths, you may have weaknesses in a variety of areas. Weaknesses, large and small, must be taken into account, especially if not considered opportunities for improvement. Remember, you don't have to hate your weaknesses. A weakness can easily be something you enjoy or want to do better — people who excel are typically not satisfied with their current state and strive to do better.

Danielle is perpetually late. She can tell you all about how much she gets accomplished because she can't walk past something and not stop to take care of it, but the fact is that she is generally late. Early in her career, Danielle became a part of a management team that required attendance at an early morning meeting. She was always the last one to arrive and was generally running from her car to drop things off in her office and rush into the meeting. After a month or so of this, it became a joke — "Danielle time." That was not a compliment. It was something she needed to change. Even today, she struggles with punctuality and considers how "Danielle time" may affect her path and fulfillment when evaluating a career step.

Examples of Weaknesses	What These Say about You
Too detail-oriented	You find that a more task-oriented role may be a good job fit and do not do well in a strategy role where you need to focus on the big picture
Perpetually late	You value your time more than other people's time and should not try to find success in an environment where you are in lots of meetings with others — a more autonomous working environment would be better suited for you
Poor at public speaking	You lack confidence or experience in the areas you've been asked to speak on publicly and work best in a supportive role where you do not have to present regularly in front of others
Unable to accept authority	You work best in the leadership position of an organization or as an entrepreneur where you can be your own boss
Not good at managing meetings	You enjoy participating, but do best when others lead and meetings are more fluid and impromptu versus planned and managed
See the <u>You Can't Eat Your Degree Workbook</u> for additional examples.	

Weaknesses based on skills you learn, such as those knowledge-based skills you are learning in college, are often somewhat easy to identify. Perhaps, for example, you didn't do so well in a writing class or a programming class so you know that is a knowledge-based weakness for you. Weaknesses in personality or soft skills may be more difficult to identify because they are subjective and not easily defined. You might not recognize that you can be perceived as abrupt because you are so focused on accomplishments and those around you may be more likely to compliment you than focus on your abruptness. If you have completed a personality assessment or seminar, you may be able to pull relevant information on your soft skills and weaknesses. If you have had a performance review in any of your jobs, use that to identify any weaknesses your manager noted.

Other ways to identify weaknesses include:

- **Take a personality assessment** to see some of your traits in a different light. They are readily available and can be found at no charge on the internet.

- **Ask someone who knows you well to share their thoughts with you.** However, it can be hard to ask someone to share what they think your weaknesses are because people don't like to share what they perceive to be bad news. So, ask for specific information, such as "I get an uncomfortable feeling at our team meetings. Have I done something to offend people?"

- **Watch people's reactions.** If you start to pay closer attention to body language and others' reactions, you'll notice when something changes the mood or alters a situation. Take note of what has happened and use that to identify a weakness.

Weaknesses do not need to be limiting factors in your career. We all have them and they are all different. Knowing your weaknesses allows you to surround yourself with others who compliment you.

Crafting Sean's Career Story: What could his weaknesses tell Sean about himself?

Sean's weaknesses:	Resulting Insight for His Career Story:
• Has an inability to see alternative pathways to a solution • Acts impatient • Can get off-track easily • Acts abrupt with team members	I'm goal-driven and want to move quickly to a solution. I thrive in an environment where goals are clear and there are direct pathways or processes to achieve the goals. I may work better as a project manager, leading the direction of an effort. I'm less interested in the relationships I build than successfully accomplishing tasks.

Explore your weaknesses. Note changes that occur in the downloadable workbook. As time passes, your core weaknesses will likely stay the same, but there will be some which you're able to overcome. The important aspect is that your career story reflects the genuine you.

Explore Inside

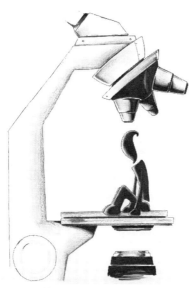

Before you can tell someone who you are or what you want to do with your future, your career and your life, you must look inside yourself, exploring characteristics, devising a standard introduction, understanding mindsets, strengths and more.

Buried in your daily activities are what you tell people about yourself, what you believe about yourself, the activities or environments you like or dislike, and your strengths and weaknesses. Bringing them to the forefront allows you to incorporate them into your future. Give yourself the time to understand who you are from both the outside view and the inside view so you can tell your career story and chart your path.

Your Trends

When analyzing a set of data, trends indicate its direction. Think about investing in a stock. Often people who try to play the highs and lows rather than ride it out are taking a huge risk. They may reap greater rewards, but the winners are few and far between. And there are likely to be as many big losses as big winnings. The safe and reliable bet is to define the trends and establish a pattern. Winners of the stock market follow patterns for steady, long-term success.

Shouldn't the same process apply to investing in yourself and in your career? If you recognize trends across the areas in the previous sections focused on defining the genuine you, then you can better direct yourself toward careers and situations that best fit your wants, needs, skills and abilities. By figuring out your trends and patterns during your college career and beyond, your degree becomes more than a piece of paper. It contributes to the picture of the genuine you and to the story you are scripting of your career path.

Finding your trends can seem difficult. That's why we start with a high-level perspective, gathering big-picture information before identifying more specific trends for a detailed perspective. You'll then begin to connect the dots between you, your trends and the story that becomes your career path.

Take a High-Level View

Taking a high-level view to find your trends means looking for those more obvious similarities across all that you do. What are the characteristics or descriptors that are consistently you regardless of setting, role or interactions? These commonalities begin to define your trends.

When Danielle recalls her career, she sees that every job she has liked has involved a great deal of human interactions. She's received compliments about her ability to build relationships and mentor people regarding careers. Her role models have encouraged her to try sales and training roles with a large percentage of time involved with interactions. Danielle's introduction generally references being involved with large groups of people and her mindsets remind her how important social activities are to her. As Danielle explores her dream job characteristics, likes and dislikes, strengths and weaknesses, she recognizes that it is imperative she incorporate large amounts of human interaction to be happy.

Which dream job aspects are present in all of the activities you enjoy? Take a look again at each of your *Looking Inside* and *Looking Outside* characteristics and consider the trends you can identify. You don't have to get specific — your high-level trends are broad and perhaps a little vague. Looking back at the areas we've already discussed, pull trends from the information you've identified about yourself. Tricia was able to make sense of her trends fairly quickly once she reviewed her dream job characteristics, likes, strengths and other recorded and significant attributes of the genuine her.

Questions to Help Identify Your Trends	Tricia's High-Level Trend Examples
Introduction: What do you consistently tell others about yourself?	Introduction: Entrepreneurial; I enjoy helping others achieve their goals; I value and encourage the benefits an engineering education can offer.
Role Models: What traits are important for you to embrace or emulate?	Role Models: Organization, planning and education are common threads; admire people who are involved in a lot of activities; people who follow their passions.
Mentors and BCFs: What types of people do you surround yourself with?	Mentors and BCFs: Smart, clever people who get things done; energetic and passionate for a cause; people who are collaborative and seek out efficiencies in their work processes.
Mindsets: What beliefs drive your decisions?	Mindsets: Education and continuous learning are important; being organized and establishing collaborations lead to better productivity and more opportunities.
Dream Job: What aspects are non-negotiable?	Dream Job: Working in a collaborative setting where I can educate others; a job that incorporates event planning and training or education.
Likes and Dislikes: What do you enjoy and desire? What will absolutely not work for you?	Likes: Working with others, planning and organizing events; leading teams; teaching; working with small teams who have connections to a larger organization or team.
	Dislikes: Budgeting and money management.
Strengths and Compliments: What do you bring to the table?	Strengths and Compliments: Connecting the dots and leveraging resources; developing curricula and training; managing complex projects, large events and volunteers.
Weaknesses and Comments: What do you need to avoid?	Weaknesses and Comments: Focus on the tasks at hand and have to remind myself to consider the feelings of all involved to ensure collaboration isn't just about work, but also about team building and interactions.

When you changed your perspective from looking outward to looking inward, did you find that your compliments aligned with the strengths you identified? Did the comments highlight areas of weakness or concern that you were already aware of, or did they highlight new areas to consider? Which trends and commonalities can you find when you combine your internal perspective with what others see in you? Which words or phrases are highlighted? Based on these trends, what do you conclude you value in a workplace setting?

By searching for trends in her career story, Tricia quickly recognized her high-level trends as education, organization and collaboration. She recognized these to be aspects of a career path she would enjoy and find fulfilling. Use your workbook or other collection method to take note of the trends you see in classes you've liked, activities you've participated in and jobs that you've had. Often, the things you liked in the classes, jobs or activities you participated in during high school will hold true in your college years and well beyond into your future. Pay close attention to your volunteer activities as they often give a different picture than a job. Volunteer activities tell you what you are passionate about, what you like to do and who you like to spend time with.

Examples of high-level trends

- Working with people
- Working outside
- Wanting recognition
- Wanting to help people
- Wanting my free time (work can't consume all of it)
- Thinking of friends as important
- Living in a warm climate
- Needing to see the results of my work

Perhaps you have a list reflective of your outgoing personality, your desire to spend time with others, or your desire to spend reflective time by yourself. Making these links will help you better understand yourself and better express yourself. And if you're having problems identifying your trends, don't forget to engage your mentors and BCFs. Those trusted outside perspectives can often help you make sense of trends easier than you can yourself.

Focus on a Detailed Perspective

A detailed perspective really focuses on the specifics across your commonalities and finishes the picture your trends paint. This detailed view gives you the clearest picture of what fulfills you and will sustain you, and helps define your career story.

For Danielle, narrowing her high-level perspective of favoring or excelling in situations with large amounts of human interaction might seem difficult. However, taking a closer look at specific situations where she has been successful and happy quickly supports her favoring human interaction and adds the details of interaction with a wide variety of people for short amounts of time. Her training and sales experiences were both great examples of this. Obtaining that detailed perspective requires that you further inspect your trends to give context to your career story — human interaction trend pops up where, when, for how long, with anyone particular, serving in a particular role?

Examples of a detailed perspective

- Working with fun, exciting people who challenge me to work harder

- Having the flexibility to work both in an office and outside on a construction site or at a minimum drive from location to location

- Wanting public recognition in the form of an improved title, verbal praise and raise from senior leadership or a manager who appreciates my strengths and perspectives that led to success

- Wanting to help people through my work to live a better life with clean water, safe communities and adequate healthcare

- Wanting my free time to be flexible so I can participate in volunteer activities that are fulfilling to me and to have my extracurricular volunteer contributions valued and recognized by my manager, senior leadership and company

- Thinking it is important to be friends with the people I work with so that I feel like I am a part of a community when I'm at work, so that I feel the support of my coworkers as a united force striving to achieve a common goal

- Being more comfortable living in a city where the temperature is not generally lower than 20 degrees and in a position for which I am not expected to go outside in cold weather

- Needing to see the physical results of my work daily — having something at the end of the day that I can look at, hold, touch and be proud of

As Tricia defined her detailed perspective, she was able to more clearly see the career path on which she needed to be. At the high-level, she had recognized education, organization and collaboration as her trends. At the detailed level, her trends became clearer.

Crafting Tricia's Career Story: What might her detailed trends say about her?

Tricia's High-Level Trends:	Tricia's Detailed Trends:
Introduction: Entrepreneurial; I enjoy helping others achieve their goals; I value and encourage the benefits an engineering education can offer.	**Education:** I enjoy working with and educating college students and young professionals. I enjoy creating and delivering curriculum for workshops, conferences and other outside-the-classroom types of environments.
Role Models: Organization, planning and education are common threads; admire people who are involved in a lot of activities; people who follow their passions.	**Organization:** I enjoy organizing large events with a variety of tasks, lots of volunteers and a clear purpose and goal.
Mindsets: Education and continuous learning are important; being organized and establishing collaborations lead to better productivity and more opportunities.	**Collaboration:** I value and enjoy working in a leadership capacity with a small team, in collaboration with leaders or teams, across a larger organization.
Dream Job: Working in a collaborative setting where I can educate others; a job that incorporates event planning and training or education.	
Likes: Working with others, planning and organizing events; leading teams; teaching; working with small teams who have connections to a larger organization or team.	
Dislikes: Budgeting and money management.	
Strengths and Compliments: Connecting the dots and leveraging resources; developing curricula and training; managing complex projects, large events and volunteers.	
Weaknesses and Comments: Focus on the tasks at hand and have to remind myself to consider the feelings of all involved to ensure collaboration isn't just about work, but also about team building and interactions.	

Tricia could see the characteristics of job responsibilities that would be most fulfilling and she began to craft her career story with these in mind.

Once you have identified your high-level trends, you will have the core information to craft your introduction and responses to what you want to be when you grow up and what your five-year goals are. A detailed perspective of your trends will help you prepare the script for your career story.

Avoid Trend Confusion

Many find trends challenging. When you are living the experiences, it is sometimes challenging to rise above the details and see the connections. If you are having difficulties finding your trends, seek feedback from your mentors, peers and BCFs.

Tricia has a group of BCFs she depends on for direct feedback and guidance. She knows they will help provide an honest perspective or constructive insights when needed. When she was offered her first position at UT Austin, Tricia was hesitant to make such a drastic career shift and turned to her BCFs for guidance. She would be leaving a well-paid engineering job with the potential for advancing in pay and title for a university position that would likely be less lucrative and potentially more limiting with her time. Tricia was focused on the disparate pay and perceived advancement limitations, but she changed her perspective when a good friend and mentor said, "You have to take the job! It's the Tricia job."

Tricia's BCF knew her career story, understood her career passions and saw the UT Austin job as an absolute career fit. Her BCF saw Tricia's trends in strengths repeated in everything she enjoyed. Tricia had not yet connected the dots for herself, but her BCF both recognized Tricia's career trends and how they aligned with this new opportunity. Thanks to her BCF, Tricia realized that pay and a defined advancement path were not the most important career aspects to her. Being in a job she loved and having the opportunity to make a difference in the lives of students every day was more important. This job opportunity was aligned with Tricia's education, organization and collaboration trends. Her friend's perspective provided her with the awareness to realize that she'd forever regret not taking that step in her career path. ∎

Don't hesitate to reach out to others for help with identifying your high-level and detailed trends. Outsiders may more easily be able to connect the dots between the characteristics, traits and aspects of the authentic, genuine, real you, and those trends can set you on the best, most fulfilling career path for you.

Your Career Story

Now that you've connected your dots and painted your picture of your dream job, it's time to sign it and create the language you'll use to communicate it. Gather the descriptors that you'll use to write your script. Use the data you gathered about the authentic, genuine real you and the trends you've identified to create your career story and then explore how to tell it.

Creating and Telling Your Career Story

Creating your career story allows you to craft the image you want others to have of you and empowers you to be proactive with your life. You'll likely repeat this cycle several times during college and your career. As experiences, passions and life situations change, your career story may also change. You should continually collect data, craft and rewrite and refine your script, modifying it as your life changes.

Collect Your Data

You have begun to collect the data you need to tell your career story. By defining the authentic, genuine, real you and identifying your trends, you have much of the data you need to prepare your introduction(s) and answer the questions about what you want to be when you grow up and what your five-year goals are. To tell your complete career story, you'll want to include information beyond what you have collected as you progressed through this book. Your complete career story will highlight those experiences and accomplishments that align with your vision of your future. By creating a system for collecting your data, including career path related experiences, trends and accomplishments, aspects of your career story will be readily available and easy to recall when you need to share them.

Can you remember what you accomplished earlier today? What about yesterday? How about ten months ago? What about remembering all those characteristics you identified earlier when reading through the *Looking Inside* or *Looking Outside* sections? It is very difficult to recall your experiences, accomplishments and career data over the past year without reminders. In the moment, it is hard to believe we can forget such a stellar accomplishment or revealing trend. Unfortunately, we often forget the most important ones when we are pressed to list them for a job interview, graduate school, award application or performance review.

Ideally, you have downloaded and used the <u>You Can't Eat Your Degree</u> workbook from 825basics.com to collect your information as you read this book. Your data should also include a thorough and flexible career history and a resume for your higher-level career data such as work experiences and accomplishments.

Record Your Career History

If you haven't updated your resume in a while or don't even have one yet, a great place to start is with a career history. And if you do have a resume already, it's easy to expand it into a career history as you will minimally have an outline to start with and easily expand. A career history is an open-ended and much more detailed resume. It summarizes your academic history, job history, experiences, achievements and skills. It's a great place to start scripting the story of your career path, interests and passions. Your career history should be encompassing, but may include whichever categories you want. Some key categories to help ensure you collect and capture everything are:

- Personal/Contact Information (name, phone, email)

- Objectives/Goals

- Academic Background (degrees, concentrations, majors/minors, specialized coursework)

- Professional Licenses/Certifications

- Work Experience and Accomplishments

- Technical/Specialized Skills

- Professional/Academic Honors and Awards

- Professional Development (conferences/workshops attended, other activities)

- Research/Scholarly Activities and Accomplishments (projects, articles, conference proceedings, books, papers presented or published)

- Grants/Scholarships/Fellowships Acquired or Administered

- Service and Volunteer Work (academic, professional, community)

- Professional Affiliations/Memberships

- Foreign Language Abilities/Skills

- All Publications/Presentations

- References

Danielle doesn't really use the categories listed above. Her career history is truly an expanded resume used as a tool to collect her experiences, skills and accomplishments in detail. Because she is unlikely to ever forward the entire document to someone or use it for a job search, she has arranged it to work for her. Danielle's career history helps her understand what she's done and where she has been. It showcases her career trends and reminds her of the career story she has and continues to craft for herself. You should arrange your career history to work for you so that it helps you prepare your career story.

It might seem like creating a career history will take a lot of time, especially if you do not already have an updated resume. So, start small. If you already have a resume, turn it into a career history by adding details and additional items as they come to mind or as you gather new accomplishments and experiences. Once your career history is created, it will be easy to maintain. Since Tricia works within the semester system for her university job, she updates her career history at the end of each semester. She wants to be sure it has the latest information. Tricia also always does a quick review of career history inclusions to see if her trends and her career path have remained aligned. Tricia's career history review at the end of each semester reminds her of her complete career story.

Starting your career history now while you are still in school will set you well ahead of most in collecting and categorizing your experiences and accomplishments. It's easier now when you're probably still in the beginning stages of producing collectable data. Also, your career history can be easier to update than your resume because you don't have to filter and limit it to only the most important career-related information.

You may never share it with anyone else, but it can be a great resource for your future. When you need to hone your script for a graduate school application, a job interview or a performance review, you'll have your past career story at your fingertips. Your career history should be the one easy place to look for your most up-to-date job, experience, accomplishment and other career story information.

Maintain Your Resume

Once you have a career history, you have the information you need to create your resume and/or keep it updated. A traditional resume is a brief, one-page summary of your relevant education, job experience and accomplishments. It is a snapshot of highlights from your career history. Brief is the key word; a resume cannot contain all of your accomplishments or every detail of every experience you have had throughout your college years and into your career. While your career history may be for your eyes only, your resume is a data collection tool that will be shared and should begin to tell your career story. A traditional resume may include the following categories similar to but not inclusive of all career history categories:

- Personal/Contact Information (name, phone, email, website)
- Objectives/Goals
- Academic Background (degrees, concentrations, majors/minors)
- Professional Licenses/Certifications
- Select Work Experience and Accomplishments
- Technical/Specialized Skills
- Recent Professional/Academic Honors and Awards
- Professional Affiliations/Memberships
- Select Publications/Presentations
- Foreign Language Abilities/Skills
- References (Listed or Statement of Availability)

Because of its limited length, a traditional resume cannot tell your entire career history or desired career path. You can't expand on each of the categories listed and keep the resume to one page. Your resume is intended to provide a good *overview* of the most important and most recent educational accomplishments and experiences. It should highlight what you value, the experiences with which you'd like future jobs to align and the characteristics of the genuine you. A traditional resume can provide an introduction or an outline to your career story.

To expand upon your traditional resume, you might consider creating a more extensive online resume. When you are not confined to a one-page hard-copy, your online resume can tell your career story in greater depth and detail. There are many ways to establish your online resume presence ranging from LinkedIn© or job boards to a personal website. Your online resume may include recommendations from others, thus providing a glimpse of the outside view of your image you explored earlier. It may showcase projects, include pictures, video or data, and provide a more complete view of what you have done and where you are headed.

Both your traditional and online resumes serve as collection bins for experiences. They should be parallel in content, with your online resume simply being an expanded version of your traditional one. They provide the high-level, most valued data points in your career history and are an additional component to the framework that is becoming your more complete career story.

Data Summary

You now have the data from defining the authentic, genuine, real you and have found your trends. With your added career history and your resume, you now have a fairly complete career story. It is documented to refer to. You can be emboldened by knowing the response to, "Tell me about yourself," and the answers to the questions "What do you want to be when you grow up?" and "What are your five-year goals?" Now you're ready to craft your script.

Define Your Script

It's time to take the information you've gathered about yourself, your data and trends, bring it together to create the verbiage you'll use to find and get your dream job. To define your script, you'll use the components of your career story that you've collected and turn them into the words to say.

At minimum, prepare your script for three situations and questions that occur frequently throughout job search and career experiences. First, the story you share when asked, "What would like to know?" in informational interviews or job shadowing situations can influence what you experience and learn about possible career paths. Next, you'll refine the career story to use when someone says, "Tell me about yourself." The third situation for which you'll define your script is when asked about your career goals.

You may never face just one of these situations or questions alone. You may face all three intermixed or incorporated in one job interview, graduate school application, or conversation with someone working in a career aligned with your dream job. The script you create will guide you successfully through these situations and questions whether they are separate, combined or thrown at you in some other way.

What Would You Like To Know?

A great way to explore career options or potential career paths is to ask people in your desired field about their job. The first thing they may ask you is "What would you like to know?" But just asking someone about what they do in an informational interview is not likely to give you the full picture of options within that degree or career path. It won't necessarily give you the information you need to determine if you'd be happy and fulfilled in a similar position. Use the information you've gathered about yourself to ask more directed questions. Some examples would be:

- I really enjoy working outside. Do computer consultants have an opportunity to work outside?

- I am great at organizing and planning events. Would that be an asset in the accounting profession?

- My professors tell me that I am highly analytical. How would I apply that skill to architecture?

- My friends always come to me for advice on technology purchases. Could I apply that knowledge and skills set to a career in the arts?

Take advantage of opportunities during college to ask people (e.g., alumni, recruiters, guest lecturers) about their careers. Your professors would probably love to share their career paths and insights with you. You may think they only know about being a professor, but they have valuable connections with professionals who practice in the areas they teach. They are likely working on projects in the field because work success outside of the institute is often required of university instructors. Ask your peers about their internship or research experiences. You have a wealth of people resources on campus to ask for career insights. You may have to seek them out, but it is well worth the effort to expand your knowledge about how your career interests can translate into real career paths and what that might mean for your lifestyle. This knowledge continues to help you craft your own story and enables you to connect your interests and passions with your characteristic trends.

Tell Me About Yourself

How do you use all this information to get that perfect job, the one that feeds you and satisfies you? Break out of the box of what is normally done in these situations and tell your story. This is best explained with an example:

Typical Method	825 Basics Method
Interviewer: Tell me about yourself. Prospective employee: I will be graduating in May with a B.S. in physics and I hope to pursue a career in research and teaching. I've been involved in the physics club, the school newspaper and I play soccer. And I am a teaching assistant in the Physics labs.	Interviewer: Tell me about yourself. Prospective employee: What I've learned in college is that I enjoy research, but I also like explaining physics to people and watching them get it. As a teaching assistant in the Physics lab, I have realized that the hands-on part of research and teaching is what I enjoy most. That's why I am a member of the Physics club and participate in our outreach program with a local disadvantaged high school. The look on the faces of these young people when they realize physics dictates so much of their daily lives is priceless. All of this has led me to pursue a PhD in Physics and a career in a teaching university. My involvement with the school newspaper has given me the opportunity to refine my writing and communications skills, which are the tools I need to effectively present my research. I'm not all work, though. I'm a member of the soccer team where I've served as the team captain for the past two seasons. I sure have learned a lot about personalities and how much each person can impact the results of a team. We've had some struggles, but our division championship last year really displayed our ability to learn from each other and begin working as a unit rather than 11 individuals. And the reward has been more than I could've expected—the championship and a community I'll be a part of for years to come, as well as the feeling of accomplishing something with the support of others.

Notice how the current method in our example is a quick synopsis of things that are likely already listed on a resume or application. The interviewer or others in your target audience already have access to these facts. What they need to hear is your story, your passion, your philosophy, the reasons you have chosen your career path. Just remember PPS—passion, philosophy, story.

> **Passion**: Who are you? What is important to you?

> **Philosophy**: How are you going to shake things up? What do you have that is unique? What perspective can you share that makes you memorable?

> **Story**: Where are you headed? Why are you the right candidate? What are you going to do to stand out?

You have all the information you need from the data you have collected as you worked through this book. Now take that data and turn it into the story you tell when asked about yourself. You craft the script to showcase the authentic, genuine, real you and can tailor it to your job, graduate school or other steps along your career path.

What Are Your Five-Year Goals?

The word *goal* scares some people and excites others. Defining goals is a process that many people start and never finish because they just don't know how to do it. The 825 Basics Method for goals starts with the authentic, genuine, real you and then works backwards from longer term goals to the more immediate or short-term goals.

You started with exploring who you are — your dream job, likes and dislikes, strengths and weaknesses. This information, the stuff you gathered in the previous *Looking Inside* section, will put you in the right frame of mind to define your goals. Now you tie this understanding of the real you into your five-year goals. Goal-setting can be challenging. By stepping back and investigating who you are and how your goals align with your dream job, you understand your career directions and can better manage your future and the answer to the dreaded interview question, "What are your five year goals?" A well-thought out answer to this question demonstrates your interest and will likely put you ahead of many other candidates. It's telling your career story in another way.

It may help to understand what a goal really is and how to write one. Your mentors, potential employers, faculty and advisors may have different definitions, but generally goals must be SMART — specific, measurable, achievable, realistic and timely.

- **Specific:** The goal must answer the 5 W's – who, what, when, where and why. You should be able to see, touch, smell, taste or hear the results of the goal.

- **Measurable:** You need to know when the goal has been achieved or how you are progressing toward the goal. There should be milestones you can track.

- **Achievable:** The goal should be attainable. It must be possible. Otherwise, why would you even want to try?

- **Realistic:** The goal should be something you are capable of and interested in achieving. Unrealistic goals would not be worth pursuing. Things you aren't interested in rarely make it to the top of your to-do pile.

- **Timely:** The goal should include a timeframe. When will you complete the task?

The more detail your goals have, the more likely you are to reach for them and attain them. Writing goals down defines them and makes them real. They provide direction and motivation for you — something to work toward, something to talk about in interviews and performance evaluations, something to discuss with your mentor or perhaps something to explore further.

Goal-setting can be broken down into eight basic steps. First, you need to define what you want or need. What is it you want to accomplish or have? You've defined much of this with your dream job scenario. Break it into smaller pieces, smaller steps on your career path that are more readily actionable. Write it all down so it becomes real and you will be more likely to hold yourself accountable. Ensure you've written it SMARTly. Review the goal periodically to remind yourself where you are headed. Check your progress and mark any milestones along the way to add to your sense of accomplishment and confidence that you can attain the goal. Revise the goal as needed, as your values or priorities change, as your organization or environments change. Finally, celebrate accomplishing your goals as you achieve them, and be sure others know what you've accomplished to reap the full rewards.

8 Steps to Successful Goal Setting

1. Want it or need it.
2. Break it into pieces.
3. Write it down.
4. Make it SMART.
5. Review it.
6. Check progress and mark milestones.
7. Revise it.
8. Celebrate it.

Your five-year goals help you move past what you can accomplish in the near future and give you time to adjust your career path, to develop skills or to make other modifications that may take time to achieve. They may be less SMART or less defined than a one-year or shorter-term goals because they are meant to bridge the gap from short-term to lifetime goals.

Once you've developed your five-year goals, break them down into smaller pieces such as one-year goals. One-year goals should take you one small step closer to your dream job and align with your five-year goals and what you know about yourself. They should more clearly set you on the path you desire. Be careful not to go overboard or overly commit yourself. Realistically think about what you can accomplish in the next year.

Consider the other commitments in your life. If you have a huge project at school, are training for a marathon and just got engaged, adding 30 one-year goals to the mix may just send you over the edge. However, if you know that these things are a part of the next year, incorporate what needs to be accomplished for prior commitments into your one-year goals. Throughout your career and your life, you will be forced to prioritize your goals, activities and aspirations. Goals could and, perhaps, should cover all areas of your life, and can generally be divided into three categories — professional, educational, and personal or family. Each category may have several goals; however, too many goals or lumping goals across categories can lead to a lack of focus.

One-year or short-term goals are necessary to achieve established milestones along the path to longer term goals. One-year goals can be broken down further to milestones throughout the year to serve as checkpoints to help you continue to progress toward your goals. Once written, accomplishing your milestones should lead to accomplishing your one-year goals, which should then lead to accomplishing your five-year and, eventually, lifetime goals. They will make it easier for you to stay focused and succeed in your career story. They may focus on what you can do this week, this month or by the end of the semester. They also allow for celebrations along the way which makes accomplishing your goals and working toward them all the more fun and rewarding.

Goals and Milestones Examples	
Five-Year Goals	• Professional: Develop a business plan for my own business. • Educational: Complete an MBA with a finance and accounting emphasis. • Personal or Family: Own my own home.
One-Year Goals	• Professional: Attain a summer internship where I can gain practical skills related to my degree. • Educational: Apply to graduate school. • Personal or Family: Put a budget together and start saving for a down payment on a house.
Milestones	• Professional: Update my resume within the next month. Determine which skills I need to hone as an entrepreneur. • Educational: Identify graduate schools by June. Take the Graduate Management Admission Test (GMAT®) in October. Get applications for graduate schools by December. • Personal or Family: Identify amount I can save each month toward purchasing a home.

To answer the question, "What are your five-year goals?" you need to be prepared with their definition and more immediate term goals to set you apart from your peers.

Typical Method	825 Basics Method
Interviewer: What are your five-year goals? **Prospective Employee:** I want to have steadily progressed in my career. I hope to be in management in five years.	**Interviewer:** What are your five-year goals? **Prospective employee:** What I've learned in college is that I enjoy serving in leadership roles within my student organizations. I have learned how to delegate and I enjoy helping others in our organization develop into leaders. As I start my professional career, I hope to obtain similar leadership roles in work and in the community to continue to hone my leadership and management skills. My goal is that in five years I will have the skills and experience to move into a managerial position, continue to grow my leadership abilities and contribute value to my organization.

Danielle has always been a goal setter. When she was in high school, she developed goals that all began with "By the time I am 30," and through this focus achieved each of these goals. But then Danielle was lost. She had been focused on the same goals for so long that she never stopped to create new milestones or a new vision for her future. Danielle spent a year with no real direction and no career story to share. When she finally took the time to set new goals and a new direction, she was revived. Danielle had a career story to tell again. Goal-setting can be difficult for all of us, even natural goal-setters like Danielle. However, once you've invested the time in yourself to set a direction, a vision, a goal, a dream, whatever you want to call it, things will seem to just fall into place.

Refine Your Script

You'll repeat this process time and time again. The questions you are asked along your career path may be the same, but you and your situation may change many times as you collect new experiences and new data about yourself. You'll use this process of defining your script in college while you are exploring career options to guide your educational path. When you are seeking jobs or graduate schools, you'll refine and use these scripts again. As your career story evolves, as you transition from one stage to the next, your script will continue to be refined so you can continuously revise and use your script to effectively communicate where you are headed.

Communicate Strategically

When corporations launch a product, the message is not left to chance. It is calculated, targeted and delivered with intention. So, why do we leave promotion of ourselves in the hands of others? Once you understand who you are and have created the scripts you'll use to answer critical questions, make sure you communicate your genuine self strategically with others. It is up to you to market yourself to your potential employers, professors, advisors and others who may influence or impact your career. Unless you happen to have your own agent like a movie star or famous athlete, it's up to you to spread the word on how fabulous you are and how you provide value.

Let your peers, friends, family, professors, managers, advisors, EVERYONE know where you want to be and what you are accomplishing. You need to market your skills and abilities and shine light on your desired career path. Get the message out there so you can excel every step along the way, and drive your career toward your definition of success. You must take charge of your career story.

Identify Your Target Audience

As a college student defining your path, take advantage of all the resources and support networks available to you. Your family should not be the only recipients of your career communications. Share your career story inside and outside school organizations with students who may either be impacted by your efforts or be part of your network. Share your story with coworkers, mentors, potential employers, professors and advisors. Your target audience should be extensive because anyone you come in contact with may be able to help you move forward.

Your peers, especially those ahead of you in their college career, can provide great insights for you. They may have experiences to share or, by sharing your interests, strengths and trends, they may help connect you with aligned job positions, potential employers and other opportunities. Seek out those students who you view as role models and request their guidance. Ask them questions about industries, opportunities, networks and connections they may know about that match with the story you have begun to write about yourself and your career path. Your peers may not only provide you with a fantastic perspective, but also resources that may head you in the right direction.

Staff and faculty are just as easily accessible on campus as your peers. They can be amazing resources for you. Tricia had a student assistant who volunteered for many years with her campus program. The student graduated without a job and was still seeking an engineering position one year after graduating. While finishing her degree, the student never mentioned her job search struggles to Tricia. The student knew what she wanted to do, but didn't use her network to help her in the process. When she finally reached out to Tricia and shared her career story — her experiences, interests, strengths and passions — Tricia was able to connect her with alumni and others industry connections that aligned with her story. In a short timeframe she was connected with a fantastic network of professionals and landed a job that has her moving forward on her career path. Had this student used her network while in school, perhaps she could have avoided the stress of the jobless post-graduation year. For the most part, staff and faculty want to help you. You just have to know what you want help with and ask for assistance. You have to tell your career story goals to ensure you get the connections and support you need.

Current and past coworkers and managers can provide a similar perspective to peers, staff and faculty. They have seen how you work and may have a better understanding of your genuine characteristics. Be sure they know your aspirations, values and goals and let them help make connections for you. They may have great insights into your career path or story and may be able to help you create or reach milestones along the way.

Potential employers and recruiters should also understand your brand and be connected to your career story. While it may seem a bit frightening to share the genuine you with those who can choose to hire you or not, it is really important to be genuine with your job search and conversations. Otherwise, you may end up in a job that does not align with the real you. You might end up taking a parallel or side step instead of a forward step toward your career goals.

Seek out these target audiences (students, peers, faculty, co-workers, potential employers and recruiters) so they can see you shine and hear your accomplishments. Your target audiences may be varied, but casting a wide net will catch more opportunities. Use your networks, promote your image and share your career aspirations. The more people who know your career story, the better.

Use Different Media

You'll tell your career story in many ways during your career. You'll share it verbally in interviews or networking settings. You'll write it out for graduate school or job applications. While each type of media or situation may require you to strategically script your career story a bit differently, you should always ensure *you* are controlling the story and the image is the one *you* define for your career path.

As you defined your script earlier, the questions considered were mostly ones you would respond to verbally. You know the phrase 'practice makes perfect?' This is absolutely true when it comes to sharing your career story and responding to the frequently asked questions that we discussed as informing your script. The more you practice the words out loud, the easier it will be for you to incorporate your career story, passions and aspirations in all kinds of settings. You'll be able to pull pieces of your story into your introduction when you meet new people, and know which segments of your story to use when the question is, "What do you want to do when you graduate?" or some other variation of "What do you want to be when you grow up?" It's your story and you should know it, but practicing it and hearing yourself say it out loud can ensure you say it with clarity and confidence in the heat of the moment or the nervousness of an interview.

Crafting your story for an application can be a bit easier since you can see it, read it and revise it before it is received. You have a spelling and grammar checker to help make sure that what you have written makes sense, at least by online dictionary standards. But it doesn't make the written version of your story any less important and you should still take plenty of time to write, read and revise to ensure it tells your career story in the way you want it to be read.

Your career history and resume are included in your prepared written career story. If they are to be shared with others to provide an overview of your career story, you need to strategically use them and make certain they have the most up-to-date and relevant information. Your resume, for example, should be crafted to align not only with your career story and desired path, but also with the organization you hope to work for or position you desire.

When it comes to social media, you'll once again want to be strategic in how and where you communicate your career story. Social media sites provide a glimpse into the personal and professional lives of those who use them. Social media can show others who you really are and what is important to you, but be careful not to reveal too much or share unprofessional or inappropriate information. Some choose to keep their professional connections confined to one site and social connections to another to help with these boundaries, but keep in mind that they are all accessible to some extent and an employer may see or be notified of anything you post online. Identify your own boundaries and use social media to help share your career story in a way that makes sense for you and where you want to go.

Your Action Plan

You are done! You have explored the authentic, genuine, real you. You have found your trends. You have scripted your career story and know how to strategically share it.

But you're not really done. The work has really just begun. You're already well on your way but have to repeat the cycle periodically to be sure your career story and path stay in alignment.

So, what's next? What can keep you moving forward to your dream job? How can you keep moving toward that fulfilling career path?

By considering what you can truly accomplish today, this week and this month, you can begin to make progress in creating and using your career story and the language you'll use to tell the world about it. It's easy to read a book, say you've got it and then jump right into the next thing. But it takes an action plan to truly embrace what you've learned about your career story and to incorporate this process into your career planning future.

Take the First Steps

Whatever your first step is, identify it. Often that is all we need, that first step, to get us moving. Define your first step for today, this week and this month on this journey to create your career story.

Perhaps your first step today is to reread a section of this book. Maybe your first step is to pay attention to what your friends say about you. Maybe this week, you'll download the You Can't Eat Your Degree workbook from 825basics.com. Maybe this month you'll start your career history. Whatever your first steps are for today, this week and this month, you're moving toward creating the perfect career fit for yourself.

So write it down. What are your first steps going to be?

Today I will: _____

_____

This week I will: _____

_____

This month I will: _____

_____

Planning is dynamic. Your actions and commitments need to be reviewed and revised on a regular basis. To truly advance toward your definition of success and that fulfilling career path, you must continually revisit, revise and reconsider what you have done and where you are going. Manage your strategy and continue to take the steps necessary to advance toward your goals. You must keep yourself in perpetual motion and your action plan constantly visible. Take those first steps today toward your career successes and fulfillment of the promises of your degree.

Revisit Your Plan

Just keeping yourself moving isn't enough. Movement is good, but if your movement is in a direction counter to your most fulfilling career path or in conflict with your values, you will have challenges. As you continue to explore, new information and circumstances may arise requiring a change of plans. Your interests may change or you may discover new likes or strengths as you navigate college and embrace new experiences. If you do not adjust along the way, you can lose sight of the environment in which you live or, worse yet, lose sight of the genuine you. Regardless of the situation, staying the course is dangerous.

We are all constantly shaped and reshaped by life and career experiences, the people we meet, our feelings, our health, our environment and our changing perceptions. Give yourself a day every year to revisit and rework your career plan. Make sure you are on the path that is important today rather than what was important last year.

This is something Danielle has been doing for years. She now looks forward to her annual quiet day of reflection and has kept every year's information in the same notebook so she is able to enjoy looking back and seeing how much she has changed. It's Danielle's career story — and it has twists and turns and mystery and drama — but it's all there for her to see and to continue to write as she progresses along the steps of her ever-fulfilling career path.